Solar Panels For Beginners

Understanding Solar Panel Technology

By

Prof. Stephen W. Bradeley BSc (Hons)

COPYRIGHT

ABOUT ME

Writer profile

My name is Steve Bradeley and I am 66 years old (2022). My name is Steve Bradeley and I am 66 years old (2022). I am an avid motorcycling enthusiast, I embrace life with a diverse blend of passions. As a writer, I try to masterfully weave together narratives that captivate readers and leave them yearning for more.

My adventurous spirit drives me to explore new corners of the world, fueling my love for travel by motorcycle. In addition to these personal interests, I remain actively interested in the realm of politics, continuously broadening my understanding and formulating informed opinions. Overall, I am a multifaceted individual whose experiences and interests make me both an interesting person. I hold a science degree from Staffordshire University.

CONTENTS

Table of Contents

BOOK OUTLINE

1. Introduction to Solar Power

   - Brief history of solar power

   - The importance of renewable energy

2. Solar Energy Principles

   - How solar panels work

   - Photovoltaic (PV) cells and their components

   - TyTypes of solar panels: Monocrystalline, Polycrystalline, and Thin-filmpes of solar panels: Monocrystalline, Polycrystalline, and Thin-film

3. Solar Power Systems

   - Grid-tied vs. off-grid systems

   - Hybrid solar systems incorporating batteries and other energy sources

4. Installation and Maintenance

   - Factors affecting solar power efficiency

   - Professional installations and DIY options

   - Maintaining and cleaning solar panel systems

5. Solar Incentives and Financing

   - Government incentives for switching to solar power

   - Financing options available for installing solar panel systems

6. Environmental Impact of Solar Energy

   - How solar energy reduces greenhouse gases

   - Recycling and disposal of solar panels

7. Solar Power in Different Industries and Applications

   - Residential homes, commercial buildings, and large-scale projects

   - Portable solar solutions for emergencies and outdoor activities

8. Future Developments in Solar Technology

- Advancements in PV technology

- Innovative applications for integrating solar power into daily life

9. Cases Studies of Successful Solar Projects

- Inspiring stories of communities that have embraced solar power

10. Conclusion: The Potential for a Solar-Powered Futur

Introduction to Solar Power

Brief history of solar power

In this groundbreaking book on solar energy, we embark on a journey through the dynamic world of sunshine power and its immense potential to change the way we live. From the humble beginnings of solar cell development in the 19th century to the cutting-edge technologies of today, this book offers a comprehensive exploration of the remarkable accomplishments and innovative advancements that have reshaped our understanding of clean, renewable energy.

The story of solar cells began in 1839 when French scientist Alexandre-Edmond Becquerel first discovered the photovoltaic effect, an essential step towards harnessing solar energy. Throughout the ensuing decades, notable figures like Albert Einstein and Bell Laboratories made significant progress in comprehending and refining solar cell technology. By tracing the milestones and breakthroughs along this incredible historical timeline, we delve deep into how increasing societal demand for sustainable solutions has driven mankind's determined quest for efficient and eco-friendly alternatives.

Through an expertly crafted narrative and engaging discussion, this book illuminates the path to the present-day landscape of solar energy, highlighting its environmental benefits, economic impacts, and transformative potential for our future. With a blend of scientific knowledge and inspired storytelling, you'll discover - or perhaps rediscover - just how far our quest for solar power has come and how it continues to shape our pursuit of a greener tomorrow.

The Importance of Renewable Energy: A Path toward a Sustainable Future

In today's world, the importance of renewable energy cannot be overstated. With the increasing concerns about climate change, finite fossil fuel resources, and the need for energy independence, investing in renewable energy sources has become a top priority for governments and industries around the globe.

In this section, we will discuss the significance of renewable energy sources like solar, wind, hydro, geothermal power and biomass, and how they contribute to a more sustainable future.

Renewable Energy: An Overview

Renewable energy is derived from natural resources that replenish themselves over time. Unlike fossil fuels such as coal, oil, and natural gas, which are finite and contribute to greenhouse gas emissions when burned for energy production, renewable sources can provide clean and sustainable power without depleting Earth's resources.

Some of the most common renewable energy sources include solar, wind, hydroelectric, geothermal power and biomass. Each of these has its unique advantages and challenges in contributing to our global energy needs. However, one thing they all possess is a massive potential for reducing our dependence on fossil fuels and decreasing greenhouse gas emissions.

Environmental Benefits

One of the most significant reasons for investing in renewable energy is its potential to reduce our collective carbon footprint. Fossil fuels release large amounts of carbon dioxide (CO_2) and other pollutants when they are burnt for power generation. These emissions trap heat within Earth's atmosphere leading to global warming and climate change.

In comparison to fossil fuels, renewable energies emit significantly fewer greenhouse gases during electricity generation. For example:

1. Solar power harnesses sunlight to generate electricity through photovoltaic (PV) panels or by concentrating solar power (CSP) technology. Both methods produce little to no air pollution.

2. Wind turbines convert wind's kinetic energy into usable electricity with minimal environmental impact.

3. Hydropower plants use water flow to generate electricity, with no air pollution and very low greenhouse gas emissions compared to fossil fuels.

4. Geothermal power plants tap into the Earth's internal heat to produce clean, stable electricity.

5. Biomass energy, derived from organic matter, offers a carbon-neutral alternative to fossil fuels as the CO_2 emitted during combustion is absorbed by plants during photosynthesis.

By supporting a transition to renewable energy, we can significantly reduce greenhouse gas emissions and curb climate change's harmful effects.

Energy Security and Independence

Fossil fuel reserves are unevenly distributed globally, with certain regions possessing abundant resources while others have limited or no access. This has led to geopolitical tensions and conflicts throughout history. Renewable energy offers a way for countries to achieve energy independence by utilizing locally available resources.

Countries with abundant sunlight or wind resources, for example, can harness these sources to produce their own energy, reducing dependence on imported fossil fuels.

This diversification of energy sources reduces the risk of supply disruptions due to geopolitical issues or price fluctuations in global markets.

Economic Benefits

Investing in renewable energy can create new opportunities for economic growth and job creation. As demand for clean energy grows, so does the need for production facilities, technology advancements and skilled workers across various sectors such as engineering, construction, operation and maintenance. The International Renewable Energy Agency (IRENA) estimates that renewable energy employment reached 11.5 million jobs globally in 2020.

Furthermore, renewable energy projects often yield indirect benefits for local communities. For instance, solar or wind farms located in rural areas may provide additional income for landowners or create new revenue streams through tourism.

In recent years, the world has been witnessing a surge in the need for sustainable and renewable energy sources. One of the most promising candidates in this field is solar energy. Solar power has come a long way since its inception, with continuous innovations driving its growth and increasing its efficiency and affordability.

1. Perovskite solar cells

Perovskite solar cells have taken the photovoltaic world by storm due to their incredible potential to improve the overall efficiency and affordability of solar panels. A perovskite is a type of mineral that exhibits unique properties ideal for solar power generation. These cells can be manufactured more cheaply than conventional silicon-based cells, providing significant cost reductions for solar panel installations.

When compared to traditional silicon-based solar cells, Perovskite solar cells boast impressive efficiency rates, with lab-scale tests reaching over 25%. This is especially important considering that commercially available silicon solar panels typically have efficiencies between 15-20%. Perovskite cells are also lightweight and flexible, making them suitable for various applications like building-integrated photovoltaics (BIPVs), portable energy solutions, and even space applications.

2. Bifacial solar panels

Bifacial solar panels are designed to capture sunlight on both sides, unlike traditional single-sided solar panels that only generate electricity from the front side facing the sun. Bifacial panels make use of reflected or diffused light on their backside, increasing their overall energy production.

Several studies estimate that bifacial solar panels can produce up to 30% more energy than their single-sided counterparts under ideal conditions. Their increased efficiency can help to offset higher initial costs and contribute significantly towards reducing the total cost of energy production from large-scale installations.

3. Concentrated Solar Power (CSP)

Concentrated Solar Power (CSP) is a promising innovation that has the potential to significantly impact the solar energy market. CSP uses mirrors or lenses to concentrate sunlight onto a small area, often heating a fluid that drives a turbine to generate electricity.

This technology can efficiently store thermal energy for later use, making it possible to produce electricity even when the sun is not shining.

There has been substantial growth in the development of CSP plants worldwide, with an emphasis on reducing costs and improving efficiency. One notable example is the Noor Complex in Morocco, currently the world's largest CSP plant—aiming to eventually generate up to 580 megawatts of electricity and store over three hours of energy.

4. Transparent solar cells

Imagine if every window in a building was capable of generating solar power. Transparent solar cells are getting closer to turning this into reality as they allow sunlight to pass through while still converting some of it into electricity. The potential applications for transparent solar cells are vast, from electronic devices like smartphones and laptops to building-integrated photovoltaics (BIPVs), where windows double up as power-generating units.

Microsoft recently partnered with Ubiquitous Energy, a company specializing in transparent solar technology, indicating that this innovation could be brought to commercial use sooner than later.

5. Energy storage solutions

Solar energy's intermittent nature requires innovative storage solutions to supply power during times when the sun isn't shining or when demand exceeds production. The development of efficient and cost-effective energy storage options enables grid operators and homeowners alike to rely on increasingly larger shares of solar power.

Some key innovations in energy storage include lithium-ion batteries, compressed air energy storage (CAES), flywheels, and pumped-storage hydroelectricity (PSH). Elon Musk's Tesla Powerwall is an excellent example of how advancements in lithium-ion battery technology are evolving.

Solar Energy Principles

How solar panels work

Harnessing the Power of Solar Energy: Understanding the Principles and How Solar Panels Work

Solar energy is an abundant and clean source of power that has captured the interest of many as a sustainable alternative to fossil fuels. By converting sunlight into electricity, solar panels give us an environmental-friendly way to meet our energy needs. To fully appreciate this powerful technology, it's essential to understand the principles behind solar energy and how solar panels work.

The Science of Solar Energy

At its core, solar energy relies on the process of photovoltaics, a phenomenon where light particles called photons are absorbed by semi-conductor materials, usually silicon. When these photons hit the surface of the material, they knock electrons loose from their atoms, creating a flow of electricity.

That flow of electricity is then captured using electrical conductors on the semiconductor's surface. Solar cells are created from these semiconductor materials and are responsible for producing direct current (DC) electricity. Multiple solar cells are connected together to form solar panels.

How Solar Panels Work: Converting Sunlight into Electricity

Solar panels comprise various layers that aid in absorbing sunlight and converting it into electricity. The essential components include:

1. Protective glass layer: A durable glass layer shields the solar cells from environmental damage while allowing sunlight to pass through with minimal reflection loss.

2. Anti-reflective coating: To maximize photon absorption, an anti-reflective coating is applied to help decrease sunlight reflection.

3. Semiconductor layers: Sandwiched between protective glass and a backsheet are two layers of semiconductor material that

have either a positive or negative electrical charge (P-type and N-type). Electrons flow between the layers when sunlight activates them.

4. Metallic grid: On top of the semiconductor layers lies a patterned grid made from aluminum or silver strips that collect and transfer electric charges.

5. Backsheet: Supporting all layers while providing insulation is a durable backsheet material.

The DC electricity produced by solar cells in the panel is then channeled through an inverter to convert it into alternating current (AC) electricity, making it compatible with household appliances and the electrical grid.

Embracing Solar Energy for a Sustainable Future

Understanding the principles of solar energy and how solar panels work highlights the potential of this renewable source in our quest for sustainable power solutions. Not only does solar energy help reduce our reliance on polluting fossil fuels, but it also provides many advantages, such as reducing energy costs and contributing to a greener environment.

By advancing research and development in solar technologies, we can move closer to a future where clean, renewable energy powers our daily lives and supports the health of our planet.

Understanding Photovoltaic (PV) Cells and Their Components: Harnessing the Power of the Sun

Solar power has rapidly gained popularity in recent years as a sustainable and environmentally-friendly energy source. One of the key elements of solar power systems are photovoltaic (PV) cells, which convert sunlight into electricity. In this article, we'll explore the various components that make up a PV cell and how they work together to harness the sun's energy.

1. The Semiconductor Material

At the core of every photovoltaic cell lies a semiconductor material, usually silicon, which has unique properties that make it suitable for converting sunlight into electricity. Depending on its crystal structure and purity, silicon can either be monocrystalline, polycrystalline, or amorphous. Monocrystalline silicon is the most efficient in terms of power conversion but also tends to be more expensive than other types.

2. The N-Type and P-Type Layers

A PV cell is made up of two types of semiconductor layers: an n-type and a p-type layer. The n-type layer is rich in electrons (negatively charged particles), while the p-type layer has an excess of "holes" created by missing electrons (positively charged regions). When these two layers are placed in contact with each other, an electric field is created at the junction between them.

3. The Absorption of Sunlight

The main function of a PV cell is to absorb incoming sunlight and convert it into electricity. As photons (particles of light) hit the surface of the cell, they may be absorbed by the semiconductor material, transferring their energy to nearby electrons. This extra energy enables some electrons to break free from their atoms and move through the material, ultimately leading to an electric current.

4. The Front and Back Contacts

Once electrons are effectively set in motion by absorbed sunlight, they must be collected and channeled into an external electrical circuit. This is where the front and back contacts come in. Typically made from a metallic material like silver or aluminum, these contacts are responsible for creating a direct connection between the PV cell and the external load, such as a battery or an inverter.

5. The Glass and Protective Layers

In addition to its functional components, a PV cell requires protective layers to ensure its durability and prevent damage from environmental factors. A layer of glass is usually placed on the top surface of the cell to shield it from debris, dust, and moisture while still allowing sunlight to pass through.

The backside may also be coated with a protective polymer or metal layer for improved stability.

Photovoltaic cells are an essential component in harnessing solar energy as a clean and renewable power source. Understanding their components and how they function enables us to appreciate the science behind this remarkable technology and continues to drive innovations in the field of solar energy. With ongoing research and development, PV cells have the potential to make a significant impact on our global energy landscape.

Different types of solar panels
Monocrystalline, Polycrystalline, and Thin-film

In recent years, solar panels have become an increasingly popular choice for homeowners and businesses looking to reduce their carbon footprint and cut down on energy costs.

With advancements in technology, there are now several types of solar panels available, each with their own unique advantages.

In this section, we'll explore the three most common types of solar panels: monocrystalline, polycrystalline, and thin-film.

1. Monocrystalline Solar Panels

Monocrystalline solar panels are made from a single, high-quality silicon crystal, which gives them their distinctive uniform black appearance. Known for their high efficiency and long lifespan, monocrystalline panels are often considered the gold standard in solar panel technology.

Pros:

- Highest efficiency rates among solar panels (typically around 15-20%)

- Long service life (often 25+ years)

- Takes up less space due to high efficiency

- Performs well in low-light conditions

Cons:

- More expensive initially than other solar panel types

- Some waste is generated in the manufacturing process

2. Polycrystalline Solar Panels

Polycrystalline solar panels are produced by melting multiple silicon fragments together, resulting in a panel with a distinct blue hue. These panels tend to be less efficient than their monocrystalline counterparts but come at a lower cost.

Pros:

- More affordable than monocrystalline panels

- Less waste generated during the manufacturing process

Cons:

- Lower efficiency rates (typically 13-16%)

- Requires more space to generate the same amount of power as monocrystalline panels

- Shorter service life when compared to monocrystalline panels

3. Thin-Film Solar Panels

Thin-film solar panels are created by depositing layers of photovoltaic material onto a substrate. They come in various forms – including amorphous silicon, cadmium telluride (CdTe), and copper indium gallium selenide (CIGS) – each with its benefits and drawbacks.

Pros:

- Most affordable option among the three types of solar panels

- Lightweight and flexible design makes them versatile for various applications

- Better performance in low-light and high-temperature conditions

Cons:

- Lowest efficiency rates (approximately 10-12%)

- Requires more space to generate the same amount of power as monocrystalline or polycrystalline panels

- Shortest service life among solar panel types (typically around 15 years)

When choosing a solar panel type for your home or business, it's essential to consider factors such as budget, space constraints, and performance requirements. Monocrystalline panels offer high efficiency and long service life but come at a premium price. Polycrystalline panels provide a more budget-friendly option with slightly lower efficiency, while thin-film panels are known for their affordability and versatility, despite offering the lowest efficiency. By understanding the pros and cons of each solar panel type, you can make an informed decision that best suits your unique energy needs.

Solar Power Systems: Grid-tied vs. off-grid systems

Solar Power Systems: Grid-tied vs. Off-grid Systems - Harnessing the Power of the Sun

The demand for renewable energy sources has grown exponentially in recent years, with solar power systems gaining popularity for their eco-friendly and sustainable nature. As more homeowners and businesses look to harness the power of the sun, it's essential to understand the differences between grid-tied and off-grid solar power systems. Let's discuss these unique setups to help you determine which option is best suited for your needs.

Grid-tied Solar Power Systems: Connecting to the Grid

A grid-tied solar power system, also known as an on-grid or grid-connected system, consists of solar panels that are connected to your local electricity grid. This setup allows you to draw power from both your solar array and the grid as needed.

One of the primary advantages of a grid-tied system is its ability to provide you with consistent electricity even on cloudy days or during nighttime hours when your solar panels may not produce energy. Additionally, surplus energy generated by your solar panels can be sent back into the grid, allowing you to receive credits on your electricity bill through a process known as net metering.

Off-grid Solar Power Systems: Electricity Independence

Unlike grid-tied systems, off-grid solar power systems operate independently from the local electricity grid. They rely solely on the energy produced by your solar panels and require a battery storage system to store excess energy for use during periods when your panels aren't generating enough electricity.

Off-grid systems offer complete independence from external electricity providers, making them ideal for remote locations or areas prone to frequent blackouts. However, they typically require a more significant investment upfront due to the need for battery storage and additional equipment.

Comparing Your Options: Grid-tied vs. Off-grid Solar Power Systems

When deciding between a grid-tied and off-grid solar power system, there are several factors to consider:

1. Cost: Grid-tied systems are generally less expensive to install and maintain since they don't require battery storage or extra equipment. However, off-grid systems can save you money in the long run by eliminating your reliance on electricity providers.

2. Reliability: While off-grid systems can be highly beneficial in remote locations or areas with unreliable grid connections, grid-tied systems provide more consistent power availability due to their connection to the local electricity grid.

3. Environmental Impact: Both grid-tied and off-grid solar power systems are eco-friendly options; however, by supplying excess energy back into the grid, grid-tied systems can contribute to reducing the demand for fossil fuels on a larger scale.

4. Energy Independence: If complete energy independence is your primary goal, an off-grid system is your best choice. Grid-tied systems still rely on the local electricity grid for power during periods when your solar panels aren't producing enough energy.

Ultimately, your decision between a grid-tied and off-grid solar power system will depend on your specific needs, goals, and location. By understanding the distinctions between these two options, you'll be better equipped to make an informed decision and harness the power of the sun to its fullest potential.

Hybrid solar systems incorporating batteries and other energy sources

Hybrid Solar Systems: Exploring the Integration of Batteries and Alternative Energy Sources

With the increasing popularity of renewable energy, solar systems have become a go-to solution for homeowners and businesses looking to lower their carbon footprint and save on energy costs. However, when considering installing solar panels, it's essential to understand the benefits of hybrid solar systems that incorporate batteries and other alternative energy sources. By combining these technologies, you can maximize your energy production, reduce dependence on traditional power grids, and even lower your long-term costs.

Understanding Hybrid Solar Systems

A hybrid solar system is a combination of a traditional photovoltaic (PV) solar system, energy storage units such as batteries, and one or more other energy sources such as natural gas generators or wind turbines. This integrated approach enables users to utilize multiple power sources based on their specific needs or circumstances.

Benefits of Incorporating Batteries

Energy storage units like batteries serve numerous advantages in a hybrid solar system. One significant benefit is the ability to store excess solar power generated during the day for use during night-time or periods of low sunlight conditions. This can help ensure a consistent power supply and decrease reliance on electricity from the grid.

Additionally, battery storage units can provide backup power during outages or other emergencies.

This added layer of security ensures that critical appliances such as medical equipment or refrigeration units remain operational even during unforeseen circumstances.

Maximizing Efficiency with Other Energy Sources

Apart from batteries, integrating other alternative energy sources like wind turbines or natural gas generators into your solar system can further improve efficiency while providing several benefits:

1. Diversifying Your Power Supply – By having more than one source of renewable energy available, you can better navigate fluctuations in power generation due to changing conditions in weather or resource availability.

2. Cost Savings – Incorporating multiple energy sources may allow users to take advantage of lower electricity rates during off-peak hours.

3. Reduced Carbon Footprint – Relying on additional renewable energy sources alongside your solar system can further reduce your overall carbon emissions, contributing to environmental sustainability.

When designing a hybrid solar system, it's crucial to consider factors such as your location, energy requirements, and budget. By collaborating with a qualified solar professional, you can develop a custom solution tailored to your specific needs and goals.

In conclusion, hybrid solar systems that incorporate battery storage and other alternative energy sources offer numerous benefits, from increased efficiency to reduced reliance on traditional power grids. As the demand for clean energy continues to grow, this innovative approach to harnessing solar power is poised to play a vital role in creating a more sustainable future.

Solar Power Installation and Maintenance: Maximizing Efficiency and Longevity

Solar power has emerged as a popular and environmentally friendly alternative to traditional energy sources. With solar panels becoming more affordable, many homeowners and businesses are looking to harness the sun's power to reduce energy costs and decrease their carbon footprint. However, solar power systems require proper installation and maintenance to ensure maximum efficiency and longevity. In these paragraphs, we'll discuss factors affecting solar power efficiency, professional installations versus DIY options, and how to maintain and clean your solar panel system.

Factors Affecting Solar Power Efficiency

Several factors can impact the efficiency of a solar power system. One of the crucial variables is the angle at which sunlight hits the panels, making installation location vital. Furthermore, shade from nearby trees or buildings can significantly reduce output. Lastly, high temperatures can affect a panel's ability to produce energy efficiently. Therefore, it's crucial to consult professionals when planning your system's installation to help address these factors.

Professional Installations vs. DIY Options

While some individuals with experience in electrical work may feel comfortable installing a solar power system themselves, professional installation is recommended for optimal performance and safety. Professionals have the expertise to assess your property for ideal placement of your solar panels, ensuring they receive maximum sunlight exposure throughout the year. Additionally, they are trained to adhere to local building codes and safety guidelines, helping prevent potential issues down the road.

Maintaining and Cleaning Solar Panel Systems

Regular maintenance is essential for keeping your solar panels working at peak efficiency over their long lifespan – typically around 20-25 years. Here are some steps you can take to maintain your system:

1. Regularly Monitor Performance: Keeping an eye on your system's energy production can help identify any unexpected drops in output – potentially indicating problems such as shading or dirty panels.

2. Keep Panels Clean: Dirt, dust, bird droppings, or snow accumulation can all affect panel performance. If possible, gently rinse your solar panels with a garden hose to remove debris. Avoid using any harsh chemicals or abrasive brushes that could damage the panel's surface.

For hard-to-reach panels or those on steep roofs, hiring a professional cleaning service may be the safest option.

3. Inspect Hardware: Annually check connectors, mounts, and wiring for any signs of damage or wear. If you're not confident in your ability to assess these components, consider hiring a professional technician to conduct regular inspections.

4. Review Your Inverter: Your system's inverter converts the direct current (DC) power generated by solar panels into alternating current (AC) used by household appliances. Inverters typically have a shorter lifespan than solar panels, so regularly check for any warning lights or error messages and replace if necessary.

In conclusion, proper installation and regular maintenance of your solar power system are essential in ensuring maximum efficiency and longevity. By considering factors affecting efficiency during installation and staying diligent with cleaning and inspections, you can enjoy the numerous benefits of solar power for years to come.

Solar Incentives and Financing

Government incentives for switching to solar power

Financing options available for installing solar panel systems

In recent years, solar energy has become an increasingly popular choice for homeowners and businesses looking to reduce their carbon footprint and save on electricity bills. However, many people are hesitant to make the switch due to the perceived high initial cost of installation. Fortunately, there are plenty of solar incentives and financing options available that can make the transition to solar power much more affordable.

Government Incentives for Switching to Solar Power

One of the most significant incentives for installing solar panels is the federal solar tax credit, also known as the Investment Tax Credit (ITC). This incentive allows you to claim up to 26% of your installation costs as a credit on your federal income taxes.

The ITC has been extended through 2022, gradually phasing down to 22% in 2023, and dropping to 10% for commercial projects only after 2023.

In addition to the federal tax credit, many states offer their own financial incentives for going solar. These can include state tax credits, rebates, grants, or performance-based incentives (PBIs). To find out what incentives are available in your area, check the Database of State Incentives for Renewables & Efficiency (DSIRE).

Financing Options Available for Installing Solar Panel Systems

If you cannot afford the upfront costs associated with installing a solar panel system, there are several financing options available:

1. Solar Loans: Many banks and credit unions offer loans specifically designed for solar panel installations. These loans usually have competitive interest rates and can be repaid over a period of several years.

2. Power Purchase Agreements (PPAs) and Solar Leases: With a PPA or a solar lease, you essentially rent your rooftop space to a third-party solar provider who owns and maintains the panels. You agree to purchase or use the electricity generated by the system at a predetermined rate. This means that you do not have any upfront costs associated with installing the panels, but you still receive the financial benefits of going solar.

3. Solar Energy Service Company (ESCO) Agreements: An ESCO is a company that installs, operates, and maintains a solar energy system on your property. Under an ESCO

agreement, the company typically receives a portion of the revenue generated by the solar panel system as compensation for their services.

4. Property Assessed Clean Energy (PACE) Financing: PACE programs allow property owners to finance environmental improvements, including solar panel installations, through a voluntary assessment on their property taxes. This enables you to spread the cost of the project over several years.

With these incentives and financing options available, it's never been easier or more affordable to make the switch to solar power. Not only will you be contributing to a sustainable environment, but you'll also enjoy significant savings on your energy bills in the long run. So why not explore what solar energy can do for you today?

Environmental Impact of Solar Energy

How solar energy reduces greenhouse gases

Recycling and disposal of solar panels

The Environmental Impact of Solar Energy: Reducing Greenhouse Gases and Recycling Solar Panels

Solar energy has established itself as a clean and eco-friendly alternative to fossil fuel-based power generation. As more homeowners, businesses, and even entire cities turn to solar power, it's essential to understand the environmental impact of this renewable energy source.

In this section, we'll explore how solar energy reduces greenhouse gas emissions and the importance of recycling and properly disposing of solar panels at the end of their life cycle.

Reducing Greenhouse Gas Emissions with Solar Energy

One of the most significant benefits of solar energy is its ability to reduce greenhouse gas (GHG) emissions. As a renewable energy source, solar power generates electricity without releasing carbon dioxide (CO_2), methane (CH_4), and other gases that contribute to climate change. The burning of fossil fuels, such as coal and natural gas in traditional power plants, accounts for a significant portion of global GHG emissions.

By opting for solar energy, we can decrease our dependence on fossil fuels, reduce air pollution, and mitigate the effects of global warming. Installing solar panels not only safeguards the environment but also promotes better public health by contributing less to air pollution.

According to research, an average residential solar panel system can offset about 100,000 pounds of CO_2 over 30 years – equivalent to planting over 2,500 trees! That is an incredible amount of pollution reduced just by choosing to harness the sun's power.

Recycling and Disposal of Solar Panels

Another aspect of the environmental impact of solar energy concerns the recycling and disposal of solar panels. Solar panels have an average lifespan of 25-30 years; after that period, they need proper recycling or disposal methods.

Many solar panel manufacturers have already implemented recycling programs to ensure their products do not end up in landfills at the end of their life cycle. Solar panel recycling includes reclaiming valuable materials such as aluminum, glass, and silicon, enabling these resources to be repurposed for new panels or other products.

In addition to implementing recycling programs, it's crucial to develop more effective and sustainable methods for disposing of solar panels.

Many countries are now adopting policies and regulations to ensure the safe disposal and recycling of photovoltaic panels.

By responsibly recycling solar panels, we can reduce waste generated by this technology. Moreover, recycling contributes to the circular economy and further solidifies solar energy's status as a sustainable and environmentally friendly power source.

Solar energy is an eco-friendly and renewable energy source that significantly reduces greenhouse gas emissions. Harnessing solar power helps mitigate climate change while promoting better air quality. To enhance these benefits, it's essential for society to emphasize responsible recycling and disposal methods for solar panels. By doing so, we can ensure a more sustainable future for Earth and generations to come.

Solar Power in Different Industries and Applications

Residential homes, commercial buildings, and large-scale projects

Portable solar solutions for emergencies and outdoor activities

Solar power is rapidly becoming a popular and viable source of renewable energy, transforming various industries and applications worldwide. From residential homes and commercial buildings to large-scale projects and portable solutions, solar power is changing the way we generate and consume electricity. In this section, we will discuss the role of solar power in different industries and applications.

Residential Homes:

One of the most common ways that solar power is used in everyday life is through solar panels installed on residential homes. Homeowners are increasingly turning to solar power as a way to save money on their utility bills, reduce their carbon footprint, and achieve energy independence. Additionally, government incentives and tax rebates have made it more feasible for homeowners to install solar panels on their roofs or even invest in community solar projects.

Commercial Buildings:

Solar power has also established itself as a valuable asset for commercial buildings like offices, retail outlets, schools, hospitals, and factories. Businesses with large rooftops or parking lots can install solar arrays to offset their energy costs while simultaneously demonstrating their commitment to sustainability. Furthermore, incorporating solar power into building design not only saves money in the long term but can also enhance a company's reputation as an environmentally conscious employer.

Large-Scale Projects:

In addition to individual homes and businesses, utility-scale solar projects have contributed significantly to the growing prevalence of renewable energy worldwide. Large-scale solar farms consist of thousands of photovoltaic (PV) panels that convert sunlight into electricity which can then be distributed to the grid. These projects play a crucial role in diversifying our energy mix, lowering electricity costs, and reducing reliance on nonrenewable resources like coal and natural gas.

Portable Solar Solutions:

Beyond traditional applications, portable solar solutions have become increasingly popular for a variety of users – from emergencies responders in disaster-stricken areas to outdoor enthusiasts seeking an off-grid adventure. Portable solar panels can be carried or rolled out quickly to provide immediate power access to devices like smartphones, laptops, and even small appliances. Solar-powered charging stations, solar cookers, and water purifiers exemplify the diverse applications of solar power for both everyday use and unique situations.

In conclusion, solar power has expanded its footprint in a multitude of industries and applications. The flexibility, efficiency, and environmental benefits of solar power have proven to be a game-changer across residential homes, commercial buildings, large-scale projects, and portable solutions.

As technology continues to advance and green initiatives gain traction worldwide, solar power's role in driving a sustainable future is undoubtedly on the rise.

Future Developments in Solar Technology

Advancements in PV technology

Innovative applications for integrating solar power into daily life

The Future of Solar Technology: Advancements in Photovoltaics and Innovative Applications

Solar power has quickly become one of the most popular and accessible forms of renewable energy, transforming the way we generate electricity and reducing our reliance on fossil fuels. As technological advancements continue to evolve, solar energy is becoming more efficient and adaptable, revolutionizing the industry through innovative applications.

In this section, we'll explore the exciting developments in photovoltaic (PV) technology and unique ways solar power can be integrated into our daily lives.

Revolutionizing Photovoltaics

Photovoltaic technology – the process of converting sunlight into electricity – has evolved rapidly in recent years, with researchers working tirelessly to improve efficiency and reduce costs. Two significant advancements in PV technology include perovskite solar cells and tandem solar cells.

Perovskite solar cells are an emerging alternative to traditional silicon-based cells, offering higher efficiencies at a lower cost. This new material has generated immense interest due to its remarkable properties, such as high absorption coefficients and tunable bandgaps, resulting in improved light harvesting capabilities.

Tandem solar cells take advantage of multiple layers of materials to capture a broader spectrum of sunlight, increasing their overall efficiency.

By combining two or more differing types of solar cells, such as perovskite and silicon-based technology, scientists can harness more energy from the sun than ever before.

These innovations in PV technology promise to further decrease the cost of solar power while improving its competitiveness with conventional energy sources.

Integrating Solar Power into Daily Life

As solar technology continues to advance, unique applications for integrating this clean energy source into everyday life are emerging. From urban planning to personal gadgets, here are some innovative ways that solar power is being woven into the fabric of our world:

1. Solar-Powered Buildings: Architects are increasingly incorporating building-integrated photovoltaics (BIPV) as a design element. BIPV systems seamlessly blend solar cells into a building's exterior, generating on-site electricity without compromising aesthetics.

This advancement not only promotes energy efficiency but also adds an artistic flair to urban landscapes.

2. Solar Roads: Pioneering projects like Solar Roadways and Wattway are exploring the potential of embedding solar panels into public roads, harnessing the sun's energy to power streetlights or even charge electric vehicles. These cutting-edge initiatives could revolutionize transportation infrastructure while contributing to global efforts to combat climate change.

3. Wearable Solar Tech: From smartwatches and portable chargers to clothing embedded with solar cells, wearable solar technology is becoming increasingly prevalent. By incorporating PV cells into everyday items, we can conveniently generate clean energy on-the-go and lessen our dependence on traditional power sources.

4. Solar-Powered Drones: Unmanned aerial vehicles (UAVs) are gaining popularity for their potential in agriculture, disaster response, and surveillance – but their need for continuous energy poses a challenge.

Enter solar-powered drones; these UAVs use lightweight and ultra-efficient solar cells to extend their operational time and reduce battery dependency.

The future of solar technology promises higher efficiency, increased adaptability, and limitless applications for harnessing the sun's energy. As photovoltaic advancements continue to break boundaries and innovative solutions seamlessly integrate solar power into our daily lives, we can look forward to a cleaner, more sustainable world powered by the sun's rays.

Cases Studies of Successful Solar Projects

Inspiring stories of communities that have embraced solar power

In recent years, solar power has emerged as one of the most promising sources of renewable energy. With its numerous environmental and economic benefits, it's no wonder that communities around the world are embracing this clean and sustainable energy source. In this part of our discussion, we'll explore some inspiring case studies of successful solar projects from different parts of the globe, proving that the future is indeed bright for solar power.

1. Solar Power in Rwanda: A Beacon of Hope

In Rwanda, a country still recovering from the devastating effects of civil war and genocide, solar power has become a symbol of hope and progress. In 2014, Gigawatt Global, an American-owned company, built an 8.5-megawatt solar power plant on a hillside just outside the capital city of Kigali. This project not only reduced Rwanda's dependence on imported diesel fuel but also supplied clean energy to more than 15,000 homes. As a result, this solar project has brought much-needed electricity to remote areas while promoting job creation and economic growth.

2. Gujarat Solar Park: Lighting Up India

India's commitment to renewable energy is evident in the development of Gujarat Solar Park—one of the largest solar parks globally.

Spread across 5,384 acres with an installed capacity of 1,000 megawatts, the solar park has played a significant role in India's transition to clean energy. Thousands of households across Gujarat now enjoy access to reliable electricity while reducing carbon emissions and bolstering India's position as a leader in renewable energy.

3. Kamuthi Solar Power Project: Empowering Rural Communities in India

Another shining example from India is the Kamuthi Solar Power Project in Tamil Nadu. Completed in 2016 with an installed capacity of 648 megawatts, it stands as one of the largest solar projects in the world. The facility covers an astounding area equivalent to nearly 60 sports stadiums and powers an estimated 150,000 homes. This project plays a critical role in India's ambitious goal of achieving 40% of its electricity from non-fossil fuel sources by 2030.

4. Tengger Desert Solar Park: China's Solar Powerhouse

China is the world leader in solar power production and the vast Tengger Desert Solar Park exemplifies this status. With a combined capacity of 1,547 megawatts, the park covers an area of approximately 43 square kilometers. Often dubbed the "Great Wall of Solar," this massive project reduces China's reliance on fossil fuels, improves air quality in surrounding areas, and showcases the immense potential of solar energy.

5. Cochin International Airport: World's First Solar-Powered Airport

In 2015, Cochin International Airport in the southern Indian state of Kerala made history by becoming the world's first fully solar-powered airport. With a solar power facility consisting of more than 46,000 panels installed across 45 acres, it generates enough clean energy to meet all its power requirements and even sell surplus energy back to India's national grid. This innovative project has inspired airports worldwide to harness solar power as a sustainable and cost-effective energy solution.

These inspiring case studies from around the world prove that solar power projects have the potential to bring about transformative change at both local and global levels. As more communities embrace this abundant and sustainable energy source, we can look forward to a cleaner, brighter future for generations to come.

What about DIY systems?

Harnessing the Power of DIY Solar Systems: An Eco-Friendly Alternative for Homeowners

In today's eco-conscious world, homeowners are increasingly seeking out ways to reduce their carbon footprint and live more sustainably. One of the most effective and popular methods is by embracing solar power as a clean, renewable energy source.

This final section will explore the basics of DIY solar systems, their benefits, and some tips to help you get started on your solar journey.

Understanding DIY Solar Systems:

DIY solar systems refer to home-built solar panels that can be installed on the roof or ground-mounted to capture energy from the sun and convert it into electricity. These systems can be customized to meet the specific needs of individual homes, making them an appealing option for those looking to move away from traditional energy sources.

Benefits of DIY Solar Systems:

1. Cost-effective: Building a DIY solar system can save you thousands of dollars in installation fees compared to hiring professionals. Additionally, you'll be cutting down on monthly utility costs by generating your own electricity.

2. Environmentally friendly: Solar power is a clean form of

energy, producing no harmful emissions or pollutants, thus making it an eco-friendly choice for environmentally conscious homeowners.

3. Increased home value: A solar system can significantly boost your property's worth, as many potential buyers view solar panels as an attractive investment that will save them money in the long run.

4. Energy independence: By generating your own electricity through solar panels, you'll reduce reliance on the grid and decrease vulnerability to fluctuating energy prices.

Getting Started with Your DIY Solar System:

1. Research your local regulations: Before embarking on a DIY solar project, be sure to check local regulations regarding permits, inspection requirements, and any incentives available for investing in renewable energy.

2. Determine your energy needs: Calculate your current energy

consumption and determine how much electricity you'd like your solar panels to produce. This will dictate the size and scale of your DIY solar system.

3. Choose quality components: It's essential to invest in reliable solar panels, inverters, and batteries to ensure the efficiency and longevity of your system. Learn about different types of solar panels and their respective efficiencies, as well as other components that will be crucial for your project.

4. Follow proper installation guidelines: Proper installation is critical for both safety and optimal performance. Be sure to follow guidelines for roof mounting or ground mounting your solar panels, proper wiring, and connecting the system to your home's electrical system.

5. Consider professional help when necessary: While DIY solar systems can be cost-effective, they may not always be the best option for every homeowner. Consider seeking assistance from professionals if you're uncertain about any aspect of your project or need help with complex installations.

DIY solar systems provide eco-conscious homeowners with an alternative way to power their homes, save money, and reduce their environmental impact. By familiarizing yourself with local regulations, determining your energy needs, investing in quality components, following proper installation guidelines, and seeking professional help when needed, you can soon harness the power of the sun and create a more sustainable future for yourself and future generations.

How do I build my own systems?

What are the components on a DIY system?

As the world becomes more environmentally conscious, many homeowners are looking into alternative energy sources to reduce their carbon footprint and save on energy costs. One of the most popular options is solar power, and with the advancements in technology, it's now possible to build your own solar panel system. In this guide, we'll explore the key components of a DIY solar system and provide some essential tips for getting started on your solar journey.

Key Components of a DIY Solar System

Before diving into the construction process, it's crucial to understand the various components that make up a solar panel system. Here are the main elements you'll need to assemble:

1. Solar Panels: These are the primary collectors of sunlight and convert it into electricity. There are different types of solar panels available in the market, with monocrystalline and polycrystalline panels being the most common ones. Each type has its advantages and disadvantages, so research carefully before making a decision.

2. Charge Controller: This device regulates the flow of electricity from the solar panels to prevent overcharging or deep discharging of your batteries. A good quality charge controller will significantly extend your battery life.

3. Batteries: Energy storage is an essential aspect of any solar system. Deep cycle batteries are recommended for solar applications because they can handle frequent charging and discharging cycles. There are various types of batteries available, such as lead-acid, lithium-ion, and nickel-iron (NiFe), each with its pros and cons.

4. Inverter: An inverter converts the direct current (DC)

generated by your solar panels into alternating current (AC) used by most household appliances. Choose an inverter that matches your energy needs and offers enough capacity for your system's output.

5. Racking or Mounting System: To safely and effectively install your solar panels, you'll need a sturdy mounting system designed for your specific roof type or ground installation.

Building Your Own Solar Panel System: Essential Tips

1. Assess Your Energy Needs: Before starting on your DIY solar project, determine your household's energy consumption. This will help you decide on the size and capacity of your solar system.

2. Do Your Research: Spend time researching different solar panels, batteries, and other components to find the best combination for your needs and budget.

3. Consult Local Regulations: Be sure to check local permitting and regulations regarding solar installations in your area. This may involve acquiring permits or adhering to certain building codes.

4. Consider Hiring a Professional: Although it's possible to build

your own solar panel system, hiring an experienced professional can help ensure that your installation is safe, efficient, and compliant with local regulations.

5. Ongoing Maintenance: Regularly inspect and maintain your solar panel system to ensure its optimal performance. This may involve cleaning the panels, checking connections, and monitoring battery health.

In conclusion, building your own solar panel system is an environmentally-friendly way to generate clean energy for your home. While it may take some research, planning, and labor, the rewards are well worth the effort. By understanding the key components of a DIY solar system and following essential tips, you can embark on this sustainable project with confidence.

Detailed instructions on How do I build my own solar panel system?

A Step-By-Step Guide to Building Your Own Solar Panel System

Solar energy has become increasingly popular as a clean and renewable source of power. With rising energy costs and growing concerns about climate change, many homeowners are considering building their own solar panel system to reduce their carbon footprint and save on electricity bills. In this blog post, we will provide detailed instructions on how to build your own solar panel system.

1. Determine your energy needs

Before you start building your solar panel system, analyze your home's energy consumption to estimate the size and capacity of the system required. Keep track of your monthly utility bills and find out how much power you need to generate to offset these costs completely or partially.

2. Investment in quality solar panels

Investing in high-quality solar panels is crucial for long-term performance and efficiency. Research different types of panels available in the market, such as monocrystalline, polycrystalline, or thin-film panels, and choose the one that best suits your needs and budget.

3. Select the appropriate inverter

The inverter plays a significant role in converting DC power generated by the solar panels into usable AC power for your home appliances. There are two main types of inverters: string inverters and microinverters. Consider factors like efficiency, reliability, and cost when choosing the right inverter for your system.

4. Acquire necessary permits and approvals if needed

Before starting any construction or installation work, ensure that you have all necessary permits and approvals from local authorities. Adhering to local building codes and regulations will save you from potential fines or legal hassles down the line.

5. Choose a suitable mounting system

There are different mounting systems available for solar panels – rooftop mount, ground mount, or pole mount. Pick an option that offers maximum sunlight exposure throughout the day while handling potential environmental factors like wind, rain, or snow.

6. Install electrical components and wiring

Once your solar panels are mounted, it's time to connect the electrical components, including the inverter, charge controller (for battery-based systems), and any required safety equipment. Make sure all wiring is done by a professional electrician, following local codes and regulations.

7. Test your solar panel system

After completing the installation, perform tests to check if the system is functioning correctly and efficiently. Measure the voltage and current output from the solar panels and ensure it aligns with manufacturer specifications. If you encounter any issues, consult professionals for troubleshooting solutions.

8. Regular maintenance and monitoring

A well-maintained solar panel system will perform optimally for many years. Keep an eye on the system's performance by monitoring its energy output regularly. Schedule periodic inspections to identify potential issues early on and maintain optimum efficiency levels.

By following these steps, you can successfully build your own solar panel system and enjoy sustainable, renewable energy for years to come. This investment not only benefits the environment but also leads to significant savings on your electricity bills in the long run. As more people adopt solar power as an alternative source of electricity, this renewable powerhouse of energy is set to play a pivotal role in combating climate change and ensuring a cleaner future for all.

Where can I buy the solar panels and equipment?

As the world becomes more environmentally conscious, many homeowners are turning to solar panels as an alternative and sustainable energy source. Amazon.com has become a go-to marketplace for DIY solar system enthusiasts looking for the equipment needed to harness the power of the sun. In this blog post, we'll explore some of the top listings and prices available for solar panels and other essential equipment on Amazon.com.

1. Best Solar Panels

When searching for solar panels on Amazon, you'll come across various types, sizes, and brands to suit your needs. Here are three highly-rated solar panels you can start with:

- Renogy 100 Watt 12 Volt Monocrystalline Solar Panel: This high-quality panel is priced at around $100 and is perfect for those starting with a small-scale DIY solar system.

- Newpowa 200W Polycrystalline Solar Panel: With a power output of 200 watts, this panel is suitable for larger projects and is priced at approximately $170.

- Jackery SolarSaga 100W Portable Solar Panel: For those on-the-go or off-grid adventurers, this portable solar panel comes at a price of around $300.

2. Charge Controllers

A charge controller plays a vital role in protecting your solar battery from overcharging. Here are two recommended options:

- EPEVER 40A MPPT Solar Charge Controller: Advanced MPPT technology ensures maximum power output from your panels. This controller is available at a price of about $190.

- Renogy Wanderer 30A PWM Charge Controller: As a more affordable option, this PWM charge controller from Renogy is priced at roughly $50.

3. Inverters

An inverter converts the DC energy from your solar panels into AC power to run household appliances. Some popular choices include:

- 5000Watt Heavy Duty Modified Sine Wave Power Inverter by Krieger: At approximately $400, this inverter is suitable for large-scale solar systems.

  – BESTEK 300W Pure Sine Wave Power Inverter: For smaller solar energy projects, this compact inverter is priced at around $50.

  –

4. Batteries

Finally, batteries store the energy generated by your solar panels. High-quality deep-cycle batteries are essential for efficient energy storage. A couple of solid options are:

- Universal Power Group 100Ah AGM Deep Cycle Sealed Lead Acid Battery: This durable battery comes at a price of around $180.

- Battle Born LiFePO4 Deep Cycle Battery: For premium performance, this 100Ah lithium-ion battery from Battle Born is priced at approximately $950.

By carefully selecting these essential components, you can successfully install a DIY solar system tailored to your power needs. Amazon.com offers an extensive range of options to build your environmentally-friendly and cost-effective energy solution.

How do I assess my electricity needs in my house when deciding how many solar panels to install?

Determining Your Electricity Needs for Solar Panels: A Comprehensive Guide

As the popularity of solar energy continues to grow, more and more homeowners are considering installing solar panels on their homes to reduce their dependence on traditional power sources and save money on energy bills. But how do you determine the right number of solar panels for your electricity needs? This comprehensive guide will help you assess your home's electricity requirements to make an informed decision about how many solar panels to install.

1. Evaluate your current energy consumption

The first step in determining how many solar panels you need is to understand your current electricity consumption. Collect your utility bills from the past 12 months and calculate your monthly average usage in kilowatt-hours (kWh).

This will provide a baseline for estimating the necessary number of solar panels.

2. Consider future changes in energy needs

Keep in mind that your energy consumption may change over time due to various factors, such as adding new appliances or electric vehicles, or changes in the number of residents in the household. Consider any potential changes in your future electricity needs and adjust your calculations accordingly.

3. Check the efficiency of your appliances

Energy-efficient appliances can greatly reduce your electricity consumption, so it's essential to factor this into your assessment. If you are planning to upgrade any of your appliances to more energy-efficient models, account for this when calculating your solar panel requirements.

4. Determine the size of your roof and available space

It's essential to consider the size of your roof and the area available for installing solar panels. Large roofs with ample sunlight exposure allow for more solar panels, which can help generate additional electricity. If space is limited, however, you may need to install higher-efficiency panels to maximize electricity production within the available space.

5. Calculate sun exposure at your location

The amount of sunlight that reaches your home plays a crucial role in determining how much electricity a solar panel system produces. Research local sun hours and solar insolation in your area to get an accurate estimation of your solar panel needs. More sun hours translate to increased electricity generation and potentially fewer panels required.

6. Factor in solar panel efficiency, system losses, and energy conversion

When determining the number of solar panels needed, it's essential to account for their efficiency, system losses, and energy conversion rates. Solar panel efficiency generally varies between 15-22%, with newer panels offering higher efficiency. Additionally, some energy (typically around 10-25%) can be lost during conversion from direct current (DC) produced by the panels to alternating current (AC) used by most household appliances.

7. Calculate the necessary number of solar panels

Once you have all the necessary information, you can calculate the number of solar panels required based on your energy consumption, solar panel efficiency, local sun hours, and energy losses during conversion.

In conclusion, assessing your electricity needs when deciding how many solar panels to install is a crucial—and very personal—process. By following these steps and considering key factors like current and future energy consumption, roof size, appliance efficiency, and location-based sunlight exposure, you'll be able to accurately determine the best solar panel system for your unique needs.

How does a Solar controller work?

A Comprehensive Guide to Solar Controllers: What They Are and How They Work

Solar power has become increasingly popular as a sustainable and earth-friendly energy source for homes and businesses. One of the essential components of a solar power system is the solar controller, also known as a solar charge controller or solar regulator. This guide will provide you with a comprehensive understanding of what a solar controller is and how it works.

What is a Solar Controller?

A solar controller is an electronic device that manages the charging and discharging process of solar panels connected to a battery or battery bank. Its primary function is to regulate the flow of electrical current to prevent overcharging, over-discharging, or any damage to the battery.

In addition, it ensures optimum energy production from your solar panels while prolonging the lifespan of your battery bank.

Types of Solar Controllers

There are two main types of solar controllers on the market - Pulse Width Modulation (PWM) controllers and Maximum Power Point Tracking (MPPT) controllers.

1. Pulse Width Modulation (PWM): PWM controllers slowly decrease the amount of power applied to the batteries as they reach full charge. They operate by sending short charging pulses to the battery, maintaining its voltage at a certain level while avoiding overcharge. PWM controllers are typically more affordable but less efficient compared to MPPT controllers.

2. Maximum Power Point Tracking (MPPT): The MPPT controller maximizes the power output from your solar panels by

continuously adjusting its input voltage based on various factors —such as temperature, sunlight intensity, and current electrical demand.

Compared to PWM controllers, MPPT technology can dramatically improve system efficiency, particularly in situations where there's limited sunlight or varying panel angles.

How Does a Solar Controller Work?

The working principle of a solar controller involves several operational steps:

1. Voltage regulation: As sunlight hits your solar panels, they generate electricity in the form of direct current (DC). The voltage generated by your panels fluctuates depending on the amount of sunlight available. The solar controller ensures that this voltage remains consistent, protecting your battery and electrical devices from damage due to overvoltage or under-voltage situations.

2. Charge management: Your solar controller also monitors the state of your energy storage system or battery bank. It adjusts the charging current to prevent overcharging, which can lead to battery damage, reduced lifespan, and even safety hazards such as fires.

3. Load control: Some solar controllers come equipped with load control features. This feature allows you to connect appliances directly to your solar controller, ensuring that they receive a consistent flow of electricity while protecting them from overloads or short circuits.

4. Data monitoring: Advanced solar controllers provide real-time monitoring of your system's performance through LCD screens or smartphone applications. These features help you track power generation, battery status, and overall system health.

Conclusion

In conclusion, a solar controller is a vital component of any solar energy system. By regulating voltage output, managing battery charging, and providing additional features such as load control and data monitoring, a solar controller ensures that your renewable energy investment operates efficiently and safely for an extended period. Whether you're planning a small residential setup or a large-scale commercial project, choosing the right type of solar contrller.

What is a solar inverter and how does an inverter work?

Understanding Solar Inverters: What They Are and How They Work

As the world continues to search for cleaner, more sustainable sources of energy, solar power has emerged as a popular alternative. One of the essential components of any solar power system is a solar inverter. But what exactly is a solar inverter, and how does it work? In this comprehensive guide, we'll explore the functions of a solar inverter and why it's crucial to the efficiency of your solar energy setup.

What is a Solar Inverter?

A solar inverter is an electronic device that converts direct current (DC) produced by solar panels into alternating current (AC). AC is the standard type of electricity used in homes and businesses to power appliances, equipment, and other devices.

Essentially, without a solar inverter, the electricity generated by your solar panels would not be usable in everyday applications.

How Does an Inverter Work?

Once sunlight hits your solar panels and generates DC electricity, that current needs to be converted into AC. Here's a step-by-step breakdown of how a solar inverter accomplishes this:

1. DC Electricity Generation: When sunlight hits the photovoltaic (PV) cells on your solar panels, electrons are knocked loose from their atoms. This process creates a flow of electrons, which generates DC electricity.

2. DC to AC Conversion: The DC electricity from your solar panels is sent to the solar inverter. Inside the inverter, there are specially designed electronic circuits that use switches to rapidly alternate the polarity of the incoming DC current. This rapid alternation creates an approximate simulation of an AC sine wave.

3. Grid Synchronization: Residential and commercial electrical grids operate at a specific frequency (50 or 60 Hz). To ensure proper function and compatibility with devices on your property, your inverter needs to match this frequency as closely as possible. Modern inverters use advanced control algorithms and microprocessors to modify their output sine waves so that they align seamlessly with the existing grid.

4. Power Delivery: Once the AC electricity is generated and synchronized with the grid, the solar inverter distributes it throughout your property. Excess electricity can also be sent back to the grid if your system generates more power than what you can use.

Types of Solar Inverters

There are three main types of solar inverters available today:

1. String Inverters: Also known as centralized inverters, string inverters are the most common type of solar inverter and are ideal for residential and small-scale commercial installations.

A string inverter receives DC electricity from multiple solar panels connected in series or parallel.

2. Microinverters: In contrast to string inverters, microinverters are installed directly onto each solar panel instead of centrally. This setup allows each panel to operate independently, providing increased efficiency and more straightforward troubleshooting in case of problems or shading issues.

3. Hybrid Inverters: Hybrid inverters are advanced models that integrate both a solar inverter and a battery inverter within one unit, enabling the user to store electricity during the day for use at night.

In conclusion, a solar inverter is an indispensable component of a solar power system, responsible for converting DC electricity produced by solar panels into AC power for daily use. Understanding how different types of inverters work can help you make an informed decision on the best option for your property as you explore the world of renewable energy sources.

What is the difference between Wet leisure batteries and Lithium Batteries?

Two popular battery options for DIY solar panel systems are wet leisure batteries and lithium batteries. In this blog post, we will examine the key differences between these two types of batteries to help you decide which one is best suited for your solar panel system.

Performance & Efficiency

Wet leisure batteries, also known as lead-acid batteries, have been around for a long time and are commonly used in various applications such as automotive and marine systems. Although they are generally inexpensive, their efficiency is relatively low compared to lithium batteries. The energy storage capacity of wet leisure batteries is limited due to their reliance on chemical reactions that occur when the battery is being charged or discharged.

On the other hand, lithium batteries offer significantly higher performance and efficiency due to their advanced chemistry. They have a higher energy density, allowing them to store more energy in a smaller space. Furthermore, lithium batteries can be discharged almost completely without compromising their performance or lifespan, unlike wet leisure batteries which require a shallower depth of discharge for optimal operation.

Life Span & Maintenance

Wet leisure batteries usually have a shorter life span than lithium batteries because they depend on the chemical reaction between lead plates and an electrolyte solution composed of water and sulfuric acid. This reaction causes corrosion in the battery over time, reducing its capacity and eventually leading to failure.

Wet leisure batteries also require regular maintenance, such as topping up with distilled water to maintain the electrolyte level and prevent damage.

Conversely, lithium batteries have a longer life span as they do not rely on fluid-based reactions that degrade over time. They can withstand many more charge-discharge cycles than wet leisure batteries without losing much capacity. Additionally, because there are no fluids involved in their operation, lithium batteries are essentially maintenance-free.

Weight & Size

When it comes to weight and size, lithium batteries have a clear advantage over wet leisure batteries. Due to their higher energy density, lithium batteries are significantly lighter and more compact than their lead-acid counterparts. This makes them easier to transport, install, and accommodate in solar panel systems where space may be limited.

Cost-effectiveness

While wet leisure batteries initially seem like the less expensive option compared to lithium batteries, considering the overall life cycle cost paints a different picture. Wet leisure batteries require regular maintenance and have a shorter lifespan, which translates into higher long-term costs through replacements and upkeep.

In contrast, the longer life span, improved efficiency, and minimal maintenance requirements of lithium batteries make them a more cost-effective choice in the long run.

In summary, both wet leisure batteries and lithium batteries have their advantages and drawbacks when used in DIY solar panel systems. While wet leisure batteries remain a popular choice due to their lower up-front cost, the benefits of lithium batteries' superior performance, longer lifespan, reduced weight and size, and minimal maintenance make them an increasingly attractive option for those seeking long-term savings and enhanced efficiency.

In Conclusion

In conclusion, solar panels offer a sustainable and eco-friendly energy alternative that can power our homes, businesses, and even entire communities. As we have explored throughout this book, the process of installing solar panels may seem daunting at first, but with the right guidance and proper planning, it is an attainable goal for anyone interested in embracing renewable energy sources.

From understanding the basics of how solar panels work to navigating the specific installation steps and procedures, this book has provided you with comprehensive knowledge on this powerful technology. As photovoltaic cells capture sunlight and convert it into electricity, you can take pride in knowing that you're tapping into a clean and inexhaustible source of energy.

As solar power systems continue to become more affordable and accessible, now is the perfect time to get started on your own solar journey. From assessing your energy needs to selecting the appropriate solar panel configuration and uncovering available incentives and financing options, you have been equipped with essential tools for success.

Remember that proper maintenance and monitoring of your solar panels will ensure their optimal performance and longevity. It is also important to stay informed about advancements in the field of solar energy to make any necessary upgrades or adjustments to your system over time.

At the end of the day, installing solar panels is not just about saving money or reducing your carbon footprint. It is about making a conscious decision to contribute positively to our planet's environmental well-being and becoming an active participant in the global shift towards renewable energy sources.

As you close this book, we hope you feel empowered by the knowledge gained as well as inspired to embark on your own solar adventure. The future is bright, and when equipped with solar panels, we can harness that boundless sunlight to light our way towards a greener and more sustainable world.

REFERENCES

The Ultimate List of UK Suppliers for Solar Panels and
Equipment

UK Suppliers

As the world moves towards more sustainable energy sources,
solar power has become a popular and efficient choice for many
homeowners and businesses in the UK. Choosing the right
supplier for solar panels and equipment is essential to ensure
top quality products, excellent service, and expert installation. In
this comprehensive guide, we'll introduce you to some of the top
solar panel suppliers in the UK.

1. Solarcentury

Established in 1998, Solarcentury is one of the UK's leading
solar energy companies, with over two decades of experience in
providing residential and commercial installations.

They offer a variety of high-quality panels, inverters, and other solar equipment from reputable brands.

2. Sun Store

Sun Store is a family-run business specializing in renewable energy systems since 2007. They provide solar panels, mounting systems, batteries, and other necessary equipment at competitive prices coupled with excellent customer support.

3. Bimble Solar

Bimble Solar focuses on offering low-cost solar solutions for both residential and commercial customers. Their extensive product range features panels, inverters, chargers, batteries, as well as DIY kits that cater to various budgets and requirements.

4. Eco Green Partners Ltd.

Eco Green Partners Ltd specializes in providing sustainable energy solutions to domestic and commercial clientele across the UK. They offer a wide range of quality solar equipment from tier-1 manufacturers such as JA Solar, Canadian Solar, and LG.

5. Midsummer Energy

Midsummer Energy is an employee-owned company dedicated to supplying renewable power system components at competitive prices. From premium to budget-friendly options, you can find an array of solar panels, inverters, batteries, mounts, and cables suitable for different needs.

6. The Greener Group

The Greener Group offers expert advice along with design and installation services for renewable energy systems. They supply industry-leading solar equipment including PV panels, solar batteries, charge controllers, and hybrid inverters.

7. Navitron

Established in 2004, Navitron is a green energy pioneer in the UK offering various solar solutions. They provide a wide range of products from leading manufacturers like Canadian Solar, Panasonic, and Victron Energy.

8. Photon Energy

Photon Energy focuses on providing high-quality renewable

energy systems for residential, commercial, and industrial sectors. With a commitment to customer satisfaction, they offer solar panels, inverters, and batteries from industry-leading brands like Q CELLS and Solis.

Final Thoughts

Solar panel technology is constantly advancing, making it more efficient and cost-effective to generate clean energy for your home or business. The list above highlights some of the best suppliers in the UK for solar panels and equipment; however, it's essential to conduct further research to find the right provider based on your specific needs and budget. Opting for a reputable supplier will ensure a seamless experience while transitioning to sustainable power generation.

United States Suppliers

In recent years, the demand for clean and renewable energy has significantly increased, and solar energy has emerged as a popular choice among environmentally-conscious consumers. As a result, the solar panel industry in the United States has witnessed tremendous growth. Whether you're a homeowner looking to power your property with solar panels or a business owner aiming to make your organization more sustainable, it's essential to know the leading suppliers of solar panels and equipment in the US. Here's a comprehensive list of top-notch suppliers to consider for your solar journey.

1. SolarWorld Americas Inc.

As one of the largest solar panel manufacturers in the United States, SolarWorld Americas is known for producing high-quality, American-made solar panels for residential, commercial, and utility-scale projects.

2. SunPower Corporation

SunPower is a global leader in solar innovation and sustainability. With over 30 years of experience in the industry, they offer exceptional solar panel efficiency, reliability, and aesthetics for both residential and commercial clients.

3. First Solar

First Solar is an international manufacturer of thin-film photovoltaic modules and a key supplier of sustainable utility-scale power plant solutions. They provide high-performance solar energy solutions for domestic and international markets.

4. LG Solar

LG Solar is a division of LG Electronics, which has been involved in the solar industry since 1985. They offer technologically-advanced and high-performance solar panels for residential installations with industry-leading warranties.

5. Panasonic

Panasonic is a well-known brand that has been providing innovative solar solutions since 1975. Their premium-quality HIT photovoltaic modules deliver excellent performance even in challenging installation situations.

6. Canadian Solar

Canadian Solar is one of the world's largest manufacturers of solar panels and equipment. With operations in North America, Europe, Asia, and South America, they supply top-quality solar products for residential and commercial installations across the globe.

7. Trina Solar

Trina Solar is a global leader in smart energy solutions, providing solar panels and related equipment for residential, commercial, and utility-scale power generation. Known for their high-quality products and advanced technology, they're a reliable choice for US customers.

8. Q Cells

Q Cells is a leading international solar company that manufactures high-efficiency photovoltaic cells and modules for residential and commercial applications. Their premier product is the Q.PEAK DUO series, which has earned numerous awards.

9. JinkoSolar

JinkoSolar is one of the world's largest manufacturers of solar panels and related equipment. They offer a wide variety of high-performance photovoltaic modules that cater to various needs of residential, commercial, and utility-scale clients in the US.

10. Silfab Solar

Silfab Solar is a North American manufacturing leader that

specializes in designing, developing, and manufacturing high-efficiency solar panels for residential and commercial applications across the United States.

These ten suppliers are just a starting point in your search for solar panels and equipment in the United States. As you explore these options, consider your specific needs, budget, and area to find the best supplier for your project. Investing in solar energy empowers you to contribute positively to both your energy bills and the environment around you.

Useful Websites

A Comprehensive List of Websites for Solar Panel Supplies

In today's world, more and more people are turning to sustainable energy solutions for their homes and businesses. One of the most popular methods is solar power, which harnesses energy from the sun and converts it into electricity.

If you're considering making the switch to solar, it's essential to know where to find reliable solar panel supplies. In this blog post, we'll provide a comprehensive list of websites that offer top-notch solar equipment and services.

1. SolarWorld (www.solarworld.com)

SolarWorld is a leading manufacturer of solar panels and modules. They offer high-quality, durable products for residential and commercial applications. Visit their website to browse their extensive range of products and find a partner/installer near you.

2. SolarCity (www.solarcity.com)

As one of the largest residential solar providers in the United States, SolarCity offers solar panel installation and leasing services. Their website provides ample information on how their system works, financing options, and incentives for going solar.

3. Wholesale Solar (www.wholesalesolar.com)

Wholesale Solar is an online retailer that sells complete solar systems, individual components, including panels, inverters, batteries, and mounting hardware for DIY installations. They also offer pre-designed systems based on your specific power needs.

4. SunPower (www.sunpower.com)

SunPower is known for its high-efficiency photovoltaic cells used in their solar panels. Check out their website to learn more about their residential and commercial offerings and request a quote.

5. Renogy (www.renogy.com)

Renogy specializes in off-grid solar solutions, offering solar panel kits for RVs, boats, cabins, sheds, and remote locations. Visit their website to shop for panels, batteries, inverters, charge controllers, solar generators, and accessories.

6. Unbound Solar (www.unboundsolar.com)

Unbound Solar, previously known as Real Goods, is a one-stop shop for off-grid solar solutions. They offer an extensive online catalog of components, including pre-designed kits, custom system design services, and installation support.

7. REC Solar (www.recsolar.com)

REC Solar provides commercial solar services and solutions to businesses, schools, government organizations, and utility providers. Their website includes detailed case studies showcasing their successful projects.

8. Soligent (www.soligent.net)

As a leading solar distributor in the United States, Soligent offers a wide range of solar products and support services. Visit their site to access their vast catalog of panels, inverters, batteries, and tools for professional installers.

In conclusion, the list above represents just a fraction of the many reputable websites offering solar panel supplies and services. Before making a decision about which company to work with, always do your due diligence – research product reviews, obtain multiple quotes, and consult with solar professionals. By taking these steps, you'll be well on your way to harnessing the power of the sun and contributing to a more sustainable future.

YouTube Channels that can help you learn about installing solar panels

A Comprehensive List of YouTube Channels for Solar Panel Installation Guidance

In today's environmentally conscious world, solar energy has gained significant traction as a clean and sustainable power source. Installing solar panels at home can help reduce your carbon footprint while saving on energy costs. If you're considering taking the plunge into solar energy, utilizing YouTube as a resource can provide valuable insight into the installation process. Here, we've compiled an extensive list of channels that can guide you in your quest to harness the sun's power.

1. DIY Solar Power with Will Prowse

Will Prowse's YouTube channel is a fantastic go-to resource for everything related to solar power. He offers easy-to-follow tutorials on solar panel installation, battery storage systems, and wiring. His experience in the field shines through in his informative and practical videos.

2. SolarQuotes TV

SolarQuotes TV is well-known for producing high-quality content about solar energy systems. The channel features expert installers sharing their professional tips and tricks for successful installations, along with insightful information about equipment and industry trends.

3. Alt-E Store

The Alt-E Store YouTube channel offers an array of informational tutorials and product reviews for those exploring solar power options. Their playlists cover topics like off-grid installations, grid-tie systems, and even wind turbines.

4. MC Electrical

MC Electrical is an Australian-based channel that focuses on residential and commercial solar installations. The hosts delve into various aspects of system design, equipment selection, and the overall benefits of going solar.

5. Solar Tech TV by RENVU

Solar Tech TV provides a comprehensive look into the world of solar panel installation, with videos covering topics such as rooftop mounting techniques, system optimization, and site analysis.

6. Solaredge Technologies

As a global leader in smart energy technology, Solaredge Technologies demonstrates how to leverage their cutting-edge technology between the solar panels and inverters to improve system efficiency and management.

7. Northern Arizona Wind & Sun

Northern Arizona Wind & Sun is an excellent platform for learning about off-grid living and sustainable energy solutions. The channel also offers advice on efficient system management, troubleshooting, and maintenance.

8. Canadian Energy

Canadian Energy's YouTube channel boasts useful information relating to solar power applications within the Canadian context. The content covers topics such as solar panel performance in colder climates and guidance on residential installation.

Through these YouTube channels, you'll gain valuable knowledge from industry experts that can help you with your solar panel installation journey. Remember to research local codes and regulations before undertaking any installations, but these resources can provide a solid foundation of understanding. Happy watching, and best of luck in your solar energy pursuits!

END

Printed in Great Britain
by Amazon

45758299R00064